Listening to the Voice of God

In the Bible we read about God speaking to many people. He speaks to Adam and Eve, Noah, Abraham, Moses, Isaac, Jacob, Rebekah, Mary, and many others.

Just as God spoke to people in ancient times, he speaks to you and me today. He speaks to us through the Scriptures. He speaks to us through other people. He speaks to us through the Church. And he speaks to us in our hearts.

Learning to listen to God's voice is one of the most important lessons we can learn in life. But learning to hear his voice clearly takes a lot of practice. One great way to practice is at Mass on Sunday. In some ways, we come to Mass on Sunday to get our instructions for the week from God.

You probably won't hear an actual voice when God speaks to you. He might speak to you through one of the readings, or through the music or homily, or he may just speak to you in the quiet of your heart.

God might say, "I want you to practice being more patient with your little brother this week." He might say, "I want you to listen to your parents and do what they ask you to do without hesitation." Or he might say, "I want you to enjoy nature while you are on your vacation this week."

God has a special message for us each week. That's why it's important to go to Mass every Sunday.

Your Little Mass Journal

God loves spending time with you. He loves it when you take a few minutes each day to talk to him. He loves it when you come to visit him at church on Sunday. He loves spending time with you. God smiles when he sees you at Mass on Sunday.

Every Sunday at Church God has something he wants to tell you.

So each Sunday, bring this little notebook with you to Mass. Before Mass begins, pray, "Dear God, please show me one way in this Mass that I can become a-better-version-of-myself this week."

Then listen, wait patiently, and when you sense the one thing that God is saying to you, write it down. Pray the rest of the Mass about how you can live that one thing this week, and ask God to help you. You will be amazed how God encourages you and challenges you to become the-best-version-of-yourself, grow in virtue and live a holy life.

There are many wonderful reasons why we go to Mass on Sunday, and one of them is to listen to God's voice.

My name is

_____

I am blessed, and God made me wonderfully and
marvelously in His own image. Jesus wants me
to become the-best-version-of-myself, grow in
virtue, and live a holy life.

God, please show me one way in this Mass that I can become a-better-version-of-myself. . .

_____

_____

_____

_____

_____

_____

_____

God, please show me one way in this Mass that I can become a-better-version-of-myself...

_____

_____

_____

_____

_____

_____

_____

God, please show me one way in this Mass that I can become a-better-version-of-myself...

_____

_____

_____

_____

_____

_____

_____

God, please show me one way in this Mass that I can become a-better-version-of-myself...

God, please show me one way in this Mass that I can become a-better-version-of-myself. . .

_____

_____

_____

_____

_____

_____

_____

God, please show me one way in this Mass that I can become a-better-version-of-myself. . .

_____

_____

_____

_____

_____

_____

God, please show me one way in this Mass that I can become a-better-version-of-myself. . .

God, please show me one way in this Mass that I can become a-better-version-of-myself. . .

_____

_____

_____

_____

_____

_____

_____

God, please show me one way in this Mass that I can become a-better-version-of-myself. . .

_____

_____

_____

_____

_____

_____

_____

God, please show me one way in this Mass that I can become a-better-version-of-myself. . .

God, please show me one way in this Mass that I can become a-better-version-of-myself. . .

_____

_____

_____

_____

_____

_____

_____

BE DETERMINED. BE CATHOLIC.

God, please show me one way in this Mass that I can become a-better-version-of-myself...

_____

_____

_____

_____

_____

_____

_____

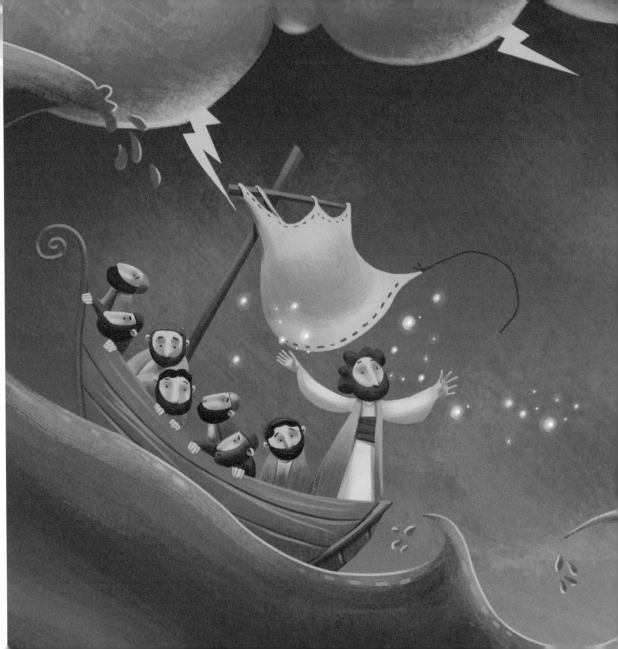

God, please show me one way in this Mass that I can become a-better-version-of-myself. . .

_____

_____

_____

_____

_____

_____

_____

BE DISCIPLINED. BE CATHOLIC.

God, please show me one way in this Mass that I can become a-better-version-of-myself. . .

_____

_____

_____

_____

_____

_____

God, please show me one way in this Mass that I can become a-better-version-of-myself...

_____

_____

_____

_____

_____

_____

_____

BE EXCELLENT. BE CATHOLIC.

God, please show me one way in this Mass that I can become a-better-version-of-myself...

_____

_____

_____

_____

_____

_____

BE EMPATHETIC. BE CATHOLIC.

God, please show me one way in this Mass that I can become a-better-version-of-myself. . .

God, please show me one way in this Mass that I can become a-better-version-of-myself. . .

God, please show me one way in this Mass that I can become a-better-version-of-myself. . .

_____

_____

_____

_____

_____

_____

_____

BE GENEROUS. BE CATHOLIC.

God, please show me one way in this Mass that I can become a-better-version-of-myself. . .

_____

_____

_____

_____

_____

_____

_____

BE GENTLE. BE CATHOLIC.

God, please show me one way in this Mass that I can become a-better-version-of-myself...

_____

_____

_____

_____

_____

_____

_____

God, please show me one way in this Mass that I can become a-better-version-of-myself. . .

God, please show me one way in this Mass that I can become a-better-version-of-myself. . .

_____

_____

_____

_____

_____

_____

_____

God, please show me one way in this Mass that I can become a-better-version-of-myself...

_____

_____

_____

_____

_____

_____

_____

God, please show me one way in this Mass that I can become a-better-version-of-myself. . .

_____

_____

_____

_____

_____

_____

God, please show me one way in this Mass that I can become a-better-version-of-myself. . .

God, please show me one way in this Mass that I can become a-better-version-of-myself. . .

God, please show me one way in this Mass that I can become a-better-version-of-myself. . .

_____

_____

_____

_____

_____

_____

_____

God, please show me one way in this Mass that I can become a-better-version-of-myself...

God, please show me one way in this Mass that I can become a-better-version-of-myself. . .

_____

_____

_____

_____

_____

_____

_____

BE KIND. BE CATHOLIC.

God, please show me one way in this Mass that I can become a-better-version-of-myself...

_____

_____

_____

_____

_____

_____

BE LOYAL. BE CATHOLIC.

God, please show me one way in this Mass that I can become a-better-version-of-myself. . .

God, please show me one way in this Mass that I can become a-better-version-of-myself...

God, please show me one way in this Mass that I can become a-better-version-of-myself. . .

God, please show me one way in this Mass that I can become a-better-version-of-myself...

God, please show me one way in this Mass that I can become a-better-version-of-myself. . .

God, please show me one way in this Mass that I can become a-better-version-of-myself...

_____

_____

_____

_____

_____

_____

_____

God, please show me one way in this Mass that I can become a-better-version-of-myself...

_____

_____

_____

_____

_____

_____

_____

God, please show me one way in this Mass that I can become a-better-version-of-myself...

God, please show me one way in this Mass that I can become a-better-version-of-myself...

_____

_____

_____

_____

_____

_____

_____

BE PRUDENT. BE CATHOLIC.

God, please show me one way in this Mass that I can become a-better-version-of-myself...

_____

_____

_____

_____

_____

_____

_____

BE PURPOSEFUL. BE CATHOLIC.

God, please show me one way in this Mass that I can become a-better-version-of-myself. . .

_____

_____

_____

_____

_____

_____

_____

God, please show me one way in this Mass that I can become a-better-version-of-myself...

_____

_____

_____

_____

_____

_____

_____

God, please show me one way in this Mass that I can become a-better-version-of-myself...

_____

_____

_____

_____

_____

_____

_____

God, please show me one way in this Mass that I can become a-better-version-of-myself. . .

_____

_____

_____

_____

_____

_____

_____

God, please show me one way in this Mass that I can become a-better-version-of-myself...

_____

_____

_____

_____

_____

_____

BE SYMPATHETIC. BE CATHOLIC.

God, please show me one way in this Mass that I can become a-better-version-of-myself...

_____

_____

_____

_____

_____

_____

_____

BE THANKFUL. BE CATHOLIC.

God, please show me one way in this Mass that I can become a-better-version-of-myself. . .

_____

_____

_____

_____

_____

_____

_____

BE TRUSTWORTHY. BE CATHOLIC.

God, please show me one way in this Mass that I can become a-better-version-of-myself. . .

_____

_____

_____

_____

_____

_____

God, please show me one way in this Mass that I can become a-better-version-of-myself. . .

_____

_____

_____

_____

_____

_____

God, please show me one way in this Mass that I can become a-better-version-of-myself...

God, please show me one way in this Mass that I can become a-better-version-of-myself...

Notes

Notes